MEGA TOP TIPS:
OFFERING THE BEST
CHILDREN'S MINISTRY

Paul Butler

Copyright © Scripture Union 2011
First published 2011
ISBN 978 184427 532 8

Scripture Union England and Wales
207–209 Queensway, Bletchley,
Milton Keynes, MK2 2EB, England
Email:info@scriptureunion.org.uk
Website: www.scriptureunion.org.uk

Scripture Union Australia
Locked Bag 2, Central Coast Business
Centre, NSW 2252
Website: www.scriptureunion.org.au

Scripture Union USA
PO Box 987, Valley Forge, PA 19482
Website: www.scriptureunion.org

Scripture quotations are taken from
the HOLY BIBLE, TODAY'S NEW
INTERNATIONAL VERSION, (TNIV) ©
2004 by International Bible Society.
Used by permission of Hodder &
Stoughton, a division of Hodder
Headline Ltd. All rights reserved.

The right of Paul Butler to be
identified as author of this work has
been asserted by him in accordance
with the Copyright, Designs and
Patents Act 1988.

British Library Cataloguing-in-
Publication Data: a catalogue record
of this book is available from the
British Library.
Printed and bound by
Bell & Bain Ltd, Glasgow.
Logo, cover design, internal design:
www.splash-design.co.uk
Internal illustrations: Colin Smithson
Typesetting: Richard Jefferson, Author
and Publisher Services

Scripture Union is an
international Christian charity working
with churches in more than 130
countries, providing resources to bring
the good news about Jesus Christ to
children, young people and families
and to encourage them to develop
spiritually through the Bible and
prayer.

As well as our network of volunteers,
staff and associates who run holidays,
church-based events and school
Christian groups, we produce a wide
range of publications and support
those who use our resources through
training programmes.

In memory of my wonderful Dad, Denys

CONTENTS

INTRODUCTION

The week in the village of Borstal, Kent was life-changing. I was helping the local Baptist church with a holiday club for local children. I was eighteen.

Since then a deep passion for the total well-being of all children across the world has grown in me. I have been privileged to work with many others who share the same passion. It has been fabulous to work with thousands of children in many different contexts. This book seeks to share this passion.

It also offers lots of practical ideas. It is written for anyone – parents, volunteers, and professionals – who longs for the welfare of children and childhood. I believe that Jesus' example and the words of the Bible offer the deepest insights available into how we view and treat all children. I write in the hope and prayer that in some small way this book may contribute to making childhood better for the children of the world.

Throughout the book, I have made many references to organisations and publications that may be of help to you. These are all listed in the Resources section at the back of the book (pages 77–79).

In writing this book I have been grateful for the immense help and encouragement given to me by Alan Charter, Andy Saunders, Mary Hawes, the Children's Advisers' Network, Keith White, Ro Willoughby and 'Tricia Williams. Above all, thanks go to my wonderful family: Rosemary, Caroline, David, Andrew and Sarah, who just keep on encouraging me.

Paul Butler

EVERY CHILD MATTERS

'I have come that they may have life and have it to the full'
(John 10:10)

Three boys came tearing through the woods shouting at the top of their voices, 'Mitchell's fallen out of a tree and broken his back!' My heart sank. We ran slithering along the wet muddy path through the woods towards the tree-house, where Mitchell had spent much of his time over the previous days of the camp. No Mitchell to be seen. We called out as loudly as we could, 'Mitchell, Mitchell!'

This was a familiar sound through the woods that week. Whenever it was a mealtime you could guarantee that the missing one would be Mitchell. When it came to bedtime, you could be certain Mitchell was still out playing. He was full of life. Aged nine, he lived in London's East End and had never before stayed in the countryside. He'd never had a chance to play in a stream, climb a tree or sleep in a tent.

He had not been easy all week – but he had been great fun. Soon, with a wide smile on his face, Mitchell appeared, running through the woods.

'Well, Mitchell, you heal pretty quickly from a broken back, don't you!' I commented. He was fine.

Mitchell will now be in his early thirties. I sometimes wonder what became of him – and whether he remembers the day he 'broke his back' in the woods of Longbarn Camp.

Think about...
Are there particular children that you recall? What makes them significant for you?

When you work with children, whether as a parent, teacher, childcare worker, playscheme staff member, children's club volunteer, nursery worker, nurse, childminder, social worker, Sunday group leader, holiday leader, or in another capacity, some children manage to make a much greater and longer-lasting impression on you than others. For me, Mitchell was one of those children.

But there were 16 other children on that camp, each with their own personalities and stories. For those of us leading the camp each one mattered, whether they were quiet, loud, athletic, adventurous, cautious or stubborn. Each one mattered to their families at home: broken, re-shaped and struggling as many of them were.

This was the first camp that my wife Rosemary and I ran for children from East London. It was a new project for Scripture Union. We led it with an enthusiastic but inexperienced team when it came to camping, though thankfully, not when it came to working with children.

Each of those 17 children provided us with encouragements and challenges. One of them returns as a leader every year, and his mum has been camp cook for twenty years. It was the smallest, one of the most difficult, yet most rewarding, of all these camps.

Establishing this camp was part of the fulfilment of the vision that had been developing ever since I started helping with children at the age of 15. The vision is all about children; their importance in the world; the wonder of childhood and the way in which, for so many, childhood is far less than it could or indeed should be.

The vision relates to the significance of children in our world, our society and within the life of the church. It was spurred by the awareness that children are often sidelined and ignored, their views and preferences given little regard by those who make decisions, whether that be in international or national politics, local communities, families or churches.

As a teenager I was captivated – and still am – by Jesus Christ's words, 'I have come that they may have life and have it to the full' (John 10:10). I want children to have life in all its fullness. It is that vision and longing which permeates all that follows in this book.

This calling to see children have life to the full has developed over the years.

Think about...
What events have shaped your involvement with children?
Is there a particular Bible verse which is significant for your vision?

It is a vision shared with many others: fellow travellers with whom I have worked and from whom I have learned an immense amount. Yet always it is children themselves who are and have been the greatest teachers and inspirers.

An African story

The lake was still, grey under the early morning clouds. Then gently, from a long way off, came the gentle 'plop' of an oar entering the water. Voices followed, not loud, but in the stillness, carrying across the waters and rebounding around the greeny-brown hills. Birds began to chatter; the smell of pink hibiscus wafted across on a gentle breeze. Lake Muhazi was looking, and sounding, wonderful. Within minutes several dug-out canoes could be seen dotted across the lake as people began their daily lives. People greeted one another as the sun rose. Before long children's voices could be heard, laughing, and calling.

I walked up the red-brown road away from the retreat centre. As I walked, watching and listening, I talked with the wonderful, living God whose creativity had brought all this into being. Soon careering towards

Think about...

'Lord, if the good news of Jesus Christ is for all people, it is for these children. Help me to consider again what you think of children, of childhood and what that does to all my theology?'

me came two children on their bikes, accompanied by two others running to keep up. No uniform, no books, but they were headed for school, still with miles to go.

Then, out of banana trees and various green plants growing on the steep hillside, a host of smaller children appeared. One, around five, was carrying her baby brother or sister in her arms. Two others were carrying well-worn yellow plastic bottles and jerry cans. They were on their way to collect water from the lake, their nearest supply. No school for these youngest; they were either too small or too busy helping with eking out a living from the small piece of land that their family worked. No parents could be seen. This might have been a child-headed household with parents lost in the war of 1991–94, the genocide of 1994 or dead from HIV / AIDS. Yet they laugh and play, and in their own way tease the passing '*muzungu*' (white person).

Think about...

Are there stories, images or experiences of children from elsewhere in the world that have made you think about your ministry? Take a look at stories about children around the world from Scripture Union International, CMS or Viva Network.

Back home

Normally, my context is England. Over the past forty years this has included many parts of London, Nottingham, Oxford, and Hampshire. I have lived amongst the poorest and the richest; surrounded by a huge range of languages, ethnic and national backgrounds; amongst churches, mosques, gurdwaras, temples, synagogues and the vast cathedrals dedicated to Money, Consumerism and Secularism. I have been involved with children who come from backgrounds of love and care, neglect and abuse, wealth and poverty and those whose family experience is mixed and varied. Any vision for children and childhood also has to make sense in this world filled with its TVs, handheld DVD players, mobile phones, Play Stations, Wii, social networking, broadband Internet, interactive whiteboards, overflowing freezers, designer clothes, international travel and wonderfully equipped schools, hospitals and leisure centres.

These different contexts explain why I cannot work with a vision for children and childhood which is confined to the United Kingdom alone. We live in a globalised world in which we are so inter-connected (even though we often do not realise this) that to think only of our own context will lead to our impoverishment.

My vision works from one simple assumption, 'Children Matter': every child matters to God, and therefore should matter to us. Whether they are the child of a member of the British royal family, a 'Traveller' in the New Forest, a factory worker in Sheffield, a top business woman in Sao Paulo, a subsistence farmer in Burundi, or a child with HIV / AIDS in India who will not survive beyond next week – they matter. Every child matters.

Being engaged in ministry with, for, to, and by children for a lifetime makes me deeply passionate about it. You cannot stay with it without a passion. It is filled with joy. It is also painful, disappointing and distressing. It still feels as though the church does not take children's ministry as seriously as it should. Institutionally, it still seems to expect it to be done on a shoestring and it remains poor at affirming those who put their heart, soul, energies and cash into it. Somehow, those who work with children and young people are still regarded as 'lesser' ministers than those who work with adults. Jesus' words, 'unless you change and become like little children' (Matthew 18:3), often remain forgotten.

But there is also a danger that those, like me, who have been engaged in children's ministry for a long time become stuck in their own ways and thoughts. Our understanding must be constantly open to fresh inspiration by the Holy Spirit, as we continually seek to be shaped by the living word of God. My prayer is that this book will trigger such a renewing for many.

FAMILIES

2

'These commandments that I give you today are to be on your hearts. Impress them on your children. Talk about them...'
(Deuteronomy 6:6,7).

There is no 'secret' for raising children who will follow Jesus for themselves. No formula or neat package can be offered that will ensure the healthy spiritual development of every child. Yet there is a hunger and longing amongst parents, and grandparents, to help their children grow spiritually as well as physically, emotionally, mentally and socially.

Think about...
In what ways do parents and grandparents express their concern for children's spiritual well-being?
Do you know good examples of work with parents?

In reality...
Parents of children attending activities at a URC church in Hackney recognised their need of help in being parents, including help with the spiritual health of their child. Almost none of these parents were church-goers.

The parents decided to meet together once a week. Whilst some 'input' from children's leaders was valued, every parent present was an 'expert'. They simply needed the space, opportunity and encouragement to listen to and learn from one another.

Help, suggestions and advice were offered for every kind of issue from sleep patterns to discipline issues. But everyone floundered when it came to helping their child spiritually. They all wanted to do this; but were not sure where to begin.

Take a look at the Bible

'Hear, O Israel: The LORD our God, the Lord is one. Love the LORD your God with all your heart and with all your soul and with all your strength. These commandments that I give you today are to be on your hearts. Impress them on your children. Talk about them when you sit at home and when you walk along the road, when you lie down and when you get up. Tie them as symbols on your hands, and bind them on your foreheads. Write them on the door-frames of your houses and on your gates' (Deuteronomy 6:4–9).

Moses' instruction is clear: make the Word of the Lord a natural part of everyday life, sitting around the table chatting, walking along the road. You do not have to force it, or create opportunities to mention God and his Word – simply build it into everyday life. The Lord of all creation is, after all, around all of the time, so talk about him naturally.

Use visual reminders

This is what Jewish believers still do; texts of Scripture, alongside visual images, act as reminders and help not only children but all of us.

Why not put up pictures and posters around your home with words from the Bible? You could also have a screen saver on the computer that includes words of Scripture or a verse which comes up when you turn on your mobile phone. In doing so, we seek to treat God's presence and involvement with our lives day by day, moment by moment, as natural, not unusual or confined to 'special' times and occasions.

A time and place

It is good to have a key time and place for specific teaching. However, if we start expecting this to be all one way, parent to child, then we miss so much. Read a Bible story together, talk about it together, recognising that the Holy Spirit will give insights to the story to everyone concerned. Let the children say what the Scriptures say to them. Do not, as parents, keep correcting them to give 'the right answer'. That is not to respect the child, or the Spirit at work. Yes, use your lifelong knowledge to help the child, but do not always assume that as the adult you are right.

Think about...
What visual images do we have around the home to help us think and talk about God?
When is a good time to read the Bible together?

'My son, keep your father's command and do not forsake your mother's teaching. Bind them always on your heart; fasten them round your neck. When you walk, they will guide you; when you sleep, they will watch over you; when you awake, they will speak to you' (Proverbs 6:20–22). See also Proverbs 1:8,9.

Proverbs offers us great insights into God's ways, especially in terms of family relationships and life. It is full of parental instruction and guidance to children. Both mother and father are equally involved. Their guidance is extremely down-to-earth and frank. It is about everyday matters like money, hard work, laziness, peer pressure, how we speak, relationships, justice in the market place, sexual temptation and much else.

Think about...

How do we talk about ordinary life and God's involvement in it with our children?

It tells us that helping our families grow is not all about teaching right doctrine and seeking to ensure children have a great grasp of the creeds (though there is nothing wrong in them having either!), but rather rooted in daily living which is marked by God's presence and ways.

'And the child grew and became strong; he was filled with wisdom, and the grace of God was upon him ... And as Jesus grew up, he increased in wisdom and in favour with God and people' (Luke 2:40,52).

Luke's Gospel, like the other three, is a carefully constructed text. So, as we read the opening chapters we hear strong echoes of the story of the prophet Samuel's birth and childhood development (1 Samuel 1–3). When later we read what happens in Jesus' home synagogue in Nazareth (Luke 4:16–30), his words about his family (Luke 8:19–21) and the stories that involve children (Luke 8:40–56; 9:37–48; 18:15–17), we read them against this opening background. The two miraculous births, and ordinary, yet extra-ordinary, upbringings with the remarkable parents (Zechariah and Elizabeth, Joseph and Mary) form a backdrop to the whole of both John's and Jesus' ministry.

The stories remind us that God has made human beings so that we all grow up in a 'fixed' pattern. None of us can evade the natural processes of physical, mental, emotional, social and spiritual development. These take place within the context of a family and a wider community who share in the privilege and responsibility of raising children so that they become adult human beings. Jesus' own life, and the example of his parents, offers us guidance and encouragement simply to help families and communities take seriously the privilege and responsibility of nurturing children.

Think about...

Read and reflect on John's and Jesus' births and childhood. Then read and reflect on the other passages in Luke quoted above. What do they say to you about childhood and the role of the family?

Practical ideas

Training and support for parents and grandparents

There are a growing number of 'Parenting' programmes available. The UK Government has recognised the importance of this and is encouraging parenting education and support. The church has produced some good resources. The best of these cover all aspects of child development, such as eating and sleeping habits, discipline, education and choosing schools, friendships and peer relationships, play, and the use of TV, computers, mobile phones and social networking.

The issues keep changing shape as children enter adolescence and the teenage years. Churches can be involved in helping parents (and grandparents who are often key carers) at every stage of children's lives. Preparing for parenthood, being new parents, early years' parenting, childhood parenting, parenting teenagers, parenting students and young adults, and becoming grandparents – all provide opportunities for churches to offer relevant support groups as a normal part of church life.

Churches can work together across denominational boundaries to run such groups. They can be open to anyone who wishes to attend: married, co-habiting and same sex couples; single parents; grandparents – all should be welcomed. The focus needs to be on

Think about...
What support is available in your locality for parents/grandparents? What could your church do?

helping parents support and learn from one another and encouraging them that they do have the gifts and abilities that they need.

Focus on the total well-being of the child which includes their spiritual well-being. This should not be as a separate 'add on', but integrated with every other aspect of the child's well-being – physical, mental, emotional, creative, social and spiritual.

Families together

Whatever 'shape' a family may have, it is important that the family spends time together on a regular basis.

Eating together

Eating around a common table, preferably with the TV off, is a great way of being together and finding out what each person has been up to. This can be a daily priority or as many days of the week as it can be done. Everyone eating at different times in different parts of the home in front of the TV or a computer game does not build family life. Have special meals together for events like birthdays too.

In reality...
One church I know encourages families to have one 'special' meal together every week. This is rooted in the Jewish celebration of 'Sabbath'. It works well.

Meals also offer an opportunity to pray together. The simple practice of saying 'grace' to thank God for the day, for one another and for the food sees the whole family praying together.

'Graces' don't need to be long – allowing the food to go cold does not enhance the family time together! They can include others not present by mentioning their names before God. 'Grace' reminds us that all things come from God's good hand.

Play and fun

Families need to play together – this might include playing a sport, simple games of chase, or board games, DVD games, Wii or just going out for a walk together. You don't need to spend lots of money on this. An occasional spending spree on a visit to a theme park is great fun, but is beyond the reach of many. It is the time spent together, not the amount of money spent on it which is valuable.

Churches can help encourage this by arranging fun events for all the family. Why not try getting together at the local swimming pool, in the local park or in the church hall? Or you could organise some fun evening or weekend activities such as dancing (eg disco, line, barn, ballroom), games, quizzes, crafts or other interests (eg sport, computer, drama, music). All of these offer ways of being together and enjoying one another's company.

Extended family times are also important, so weekends away and holidays are invaluable. Churches can help and enhance this by running their own times away for families together. Be enterprising by choosing a venue where some can camp, whilst others are in a house or hotel. Or, you could join in with family-geared holidays run at places like Lee Abbey, Great Wood or larger events like Spring Harvest, New Wine and Walsingham.

Play is important for everyone. Playing and having fun together helps build family life.

Dads and lads / mums and daughters

It is also very valuable for parents to spend one-to-one time with individual children. This can be as simple as going off for a walk together, going fishing, going to see a film, shopping, tenpin bowling, having a make-up session, or watching a football match. Your church could also organise specific events or activities where dads and their sons, or mums and their daughters can get away together for some energetic or creative activities and simply to enjoy one another's company. It builds the relationship and strengthens family life. Some YMCAs, local Youth for Christ groups, retreat and activity centres have developed good programmes with these kinds of events in mind.

Think about…

Reflect on the ideas above. How is your church already engaging in ways like this? Are there things that could be improved or started? How?

Single-parent events

Churches are full of 'single' parents, yet often people can have the feeling that the church is really only for two-parent families. Somehow that image has to be changed, and

In reality…

A church in Bournemouth arranged a day specifically for single-parent families. Church members offered their time and skills for the day. They helped get jobs sorted in people's homes, offered activities, skills training, free 'pampering' sessions, great children's activities and good food. It was all done entirely by church members donating their time and skills for the day.

churches will be seen to be places where all types of families are welcome and cared for.

Churches need to think through how they can offer support to single parents. For example:

- offer childcare so that Dad or Mum can have an evening out, or get to a 'home group'
- run daytime groups with childcare available, or where the children play happily as parents chat, look at the Bible together and pray
- offer parents'/carers' groups and toddler groups
- hold midweek services that are toddler-friendly

All these can offer space and a place for single parents to be involved, to feel welcomed, to be helped to worship and to learn about the Christian faith in a setting where their children are doing the same.

A family-friendly church will always be a single-parent, family-friendly church.

Broken families

All the statistics indicate that more and more children experience being a part of a 'broken' family. Parents (whether co-habiting or married) split up, and children are affected. Sadly some children experience abuse (neglect, emotional, physical, sexual and spiritual) from their parents and it affects them for life. Yet children are also remarkably resilient and handle this brokenness; some come through it deeply scarred while others somehow come through apparently almost unscathed.

Local churches are not immune from all of this. Sadly, marriages fail as often in church families as in society as a whole. Tragically children are abused in Christian families; sometimes they are even neglected 'for the sake of the ministry'. So churches need to engage in teaching

Think about...
How is our church helping
families handle 'brokenness'?

about family life; they need to be places where grace and forgiveness flow when problems and brokenness arise. Churches can provide safe spaces for separated children to meet up with the estranged parent on neutral ground. Churches can provide counselling and support, and can be places of healing and restoration for children and their families.

Praying as families

We have already noted the value of a time and place, saying grace and talking naturally about God and his Word together.

Finding the right time may well depend on a child's own energy and sleep patterns. It might be good at the beginning, or end of the day. Somewhere in the middle of the morning or after lunch might work well when the child is small. Find the best place, and don't be afraid to change it with the years as lifestyle and patterns change with pre-school, nursery, school etc. Reading a small part of the Bible together, talking about it and then a few short prayers, probably including the Lord's Prayer, is all that is needed.

This may only last a few minutes or take longer. You could follow this up with a creative activity based on the story (painting or drawing a picture; modelling something in dough or clay; writing something together). Don't shy away from using the text of the Bible, even with the smallest child. Toddlers' and children's Bibles have their place – the pictures and simpler words can help. But there is no substitute for the words of Scripture themselves. Get hold of *The Bible (Narrative & Illustrated)*, WTL Bible Publications with its wonderful colour pictures on every page. Let the Bible speak for itself to everyone in the family. Remember the youngest child's response and reflection may be the insight from the Holy Spirit that all members of the family need to hear.

Wrapping it up

Think about...
Reflect on the ideas above. How is your church already engaging in ways like this? Are there things that could be improved or started? How?

Every child is part of their family. Some of those families are broken and dysfunctional. We cannot work for the well-being of the child apart from their family context. The church should continue to teach that life-long marriage between a man and a woman is the best setting for children to be raised. Yet, at the same time, it must work positively and openly with all children and all families, whatever their make up, especially when they become broken.

3

SCHOOL

'The fear of the Lord is the beginning of knowledge, but fools despise wisdom and instruction' (Proverbs 1:7).

In reality...

The school hall was crowded. Children aged five to eleven were excitedly eating breakfast, talking, reading and playing games. The Breakfast Club was in full swing. The numbers were higher than usual because BBC Radio Solent were present broadcasting parts of their early morning programme from the school. The highlight was the bacon tasting test. It was great fun with the local butcher winning hands down.

After it was all done, school began properly. I took part in the collective worship. Then, with the head teacher, some of the children and the local vicar, we set off walking through the parish in the rain and mud. It was a wonderful three hours sharing in their lives, as they shared in my 'prayer walk' across the area.

One of Tony Blair's most memorable speeches began 'Education, education, education.' In the past ten years large sums of money have been invested in education at every level. There have been, and continue to be, many changes in the curriculum, the role of national and local government, the nature of schools, inspection regimes and the role and responsibilities of head teachers, staff, parents, communities and governors. A strong commitment to education by all political parties is clear.

On the world scene the second of the United Nations Millennium Development Goals is 'Universal Primary Education'. The goal is to *'ensure that, by 2015, children everywhere, boys and girls alike, will be able to complete a full course of primary schooling'.* Throughout the world there is a recognition that education matters and needs to be given priority.

Think about... How has education changed in your own locality over the past decade?

The Church has been engaged in education for a very long time. Many schools in Britain have a church foundation. Around the world the church is deeply engaged in education. Education for the poorest has been at the forefront of many of the churches' initiatives through the centuries. Robert Raikes first established his 'Sunday School' in 1780 to be a means of helping the children of the poor to learn to read and write, so that they could come to read the Bible for themselves. On 16th October 1811 The National Society for Promoting Religious Education was founded with the express purpose 'That the National Religion should be made the foundation of National Education, and should be the first and chief thing taught to the poor, according to the excellent Liturgy and Catechism provided by our Church.' The Society's mission was to found a church school in every parish in England and Wales. In various ways, the church's involvement has continued ever since. At the present time:

- Around 25% of all state primary schools in England are Church of England schools – 4,470 schools.
- Around 6% of all state secondary schools in England are Church of England schools – 220 schools. Further growth is planned over the next few years.
- Many new academies have a Christian foundation.
- Catholic primary, secondary and independent schools and sixth form colleges serve the needs of 840,000 children and young

people in England and Wales; just under 10% of the total school population.

- Additionally within the independent sector there are many whose foundation is Anglican. Then there are places of higher education and universities whose foundation lies in the Church of England, Roman Catholic Church or Free churches.

In reality...

The Church of Uganda is responsible for large numbers of schools in cities, towns and some of the remotest and poorest communities. It engages fully in higher education through the Uganda Christian University. The story is repeated through churches of different denominations across Africa, through South and Central America, in India, Pakistan and South East Asia.

There has also been an enormous growth over the past four to five decades in early years' education. This began in the United Kingdom with the Play Group movement of the 1960s and has expanded through the development of nursery schools and pre-school groups. Many of these continue to have connections with local churches, either being run by churches themselves, or being run in church property.

With the continued place of Sunday Schools, children's and young

Think about...
What resources do local churches in your area put into all stages of education?

people's groups, and engagement with all types of schools in a host of ways, the church's time and energy put into education, both formal and informal, is enormous. There can be no question that the church is strongly committed to education.

Take a look at the Bible

We do not find today's educational activities and institutions in the pages of the Bible. What we do find is a people who were passionate about passing on their history, culture and faith to the next generations (Psalm 78). We find a hunger for knowledge and wisdom, rooted in 'the fear of the Lord' (Proverbs 1). We find some deeply committed to learning and study, like the rabbis and their scribes. We know from extra biblical literature that in the time of the exile in Babylon, and thereafter, the Jews developed 'schools' based in the synagogues. In these, boys from around six until thirteen, learned to read and write the Hebrew language. This was primarily so that they could read and learn the Scriptures. Jesus would have attended such a synagogue school in Nazareth. It is likely that he spoke Aramaic most of the time but could read, and quote, the Hebrew Scriptures. It is also quite possible that through his trading as a carpenter in northern Israel he picked up at least some Greek, and possibly Latin as well.

So what is education for? Why does the church want to engage with schools?

The book of Proverbs contains many sayings about wisdom, knowledge and learning. At its outset it has a very clear summary about its own purpose, and where true knowledge lies.

'For gaining wisdom and instruction; for understanding words of insight; for receiving instruction in prudent behaviour, doing what is

right and just and fair; for giving prudence to those who are simple, knowledge and discretion to the young – let the wise listen and add to their learning, and let the discerning get guidance – for understanding proverbs and parables, the sayings and riddles of the wise. The fear of the Lord is the beginning of knowledge, but fools despise wisdom and instruction' (Proverbs 1:2–7).

Instruction and learning, according to the writer, are about gaining wisdom for life; they are about enabling people to make right judgements and seek justice in our world. The heart of learning is found in reverence for 'the Lord'. Holy awe, due humility and openness to the Creator God and his ways lie at the heart of true knowledge and learning.

So education is primarily concerned about learning for life. It has a spiritual heart to it. It is deeply concerned about morality and wisdom for living in community with others. These are the priorities of the writer of Proverbs. Knowledge must have a purpose; it is not simply knowledge for knowledge's sake but so we know how to live. Now this is of vital importance to our understanding about education, and our priorities for it. This offers us a vision for engaging with pre-schools, nurseries, schools and all other educational establishments.

Think about...
What do you think education is for?

Practical ideas

Prayer for schools
All churches should be praying regularly for their local pre-schools, nurseries, schools and colleges. Encourage people to include them in

their own prayers; include them in public intercessions during worship; put items for prayer in church notice-sheets and magazines. There is a place for a dedicated prayer group for each local school, or group of schools. A home or cell group could take on the responsibility for praying for a particular school. Let the school know this is happening; hold the prayer group in the school if possible. Simply ask the school for any particular concerns about which to pray. Even if the response is negative or lukewarm, keep praying.

Think about...
How are schools prayed for in your church? What could be done to develop this further?

Helping out

Schools are always looking for people who will help them. Activities might include help with listening to children read; assisting with trips out of school; art, craft, and cookery activities and keeping the school library in order.

The Extended Schools Agenda means that all schools are exploring what kind of provision they can make for children before and after school. Breakfast clubs guarantee a good start to the day for many children. After-school activities take many forms: homework clubs, language groups, sport, craft and much else besides. These activities sometimes involve teachers but they are often overstretched and struggle to find the time and energy, so many are run by other providers.

There is every reason why local churches should explore organising and running these themselves or in partnership with an organisation like the YMCA. One local minister I know runs the school gardening club; someone else runs a choir. Then there are overtly Christian lunchtime or after-school Bible-based groups, often using Scripture Union's SchoolsLive materials.

In the school holidays church teams can help sort out school grounds, paint classrooms, and shift furniture. Just offer to help, with no agenda other than serving the school in the name of Christ.

Think about...
What help does your church currently offer? Are there fresh areas of help that could be offered?

School 'worship'

The law is still clear that there should be a daily act of worship in every school, and that this should be 'broadly, mainly Christian' (unless a school has received a 'determination' from a local authority that it can supply a range of worship for different faith communities). In church schools the worship should naturally reflect the Christian foundation, but all schools should be holding some kind of act of worship. So local clergy, and other able church leaders, should be offering to help with this aspect of school life in all types of schools. Such leading should always be done in clear consultation with the head teacher and should respect the school's policies. If the 'assembly' lasts five minutes, it is impolite to overrun. If prayer is not the norm then respect this. But Christian leaders should never be ashamed of being open about their own Christian faith. School 'worship' is not a base for evangelism, but it is a base for modelling Christian worship and living. There is plenty of scope for developing a team of people to assist with musical, dramatic, dance and other skills. School worship is not meant to be entertainment but it should be entertaining; it is not a comedy show but it can certainly be humorous. The one thing it should not be is boring!

Then there is the possibility of the school visiting the church for an act of worship, for example: Harvest, Christmas, Easter and for Leavers' services at the end of the year (even better if that could be tied in with SU's 'It's your move' materials). Many schools that are not church schools value such opportunities. Make them happen.

Think about...
Who engages with local school worship at present? How? Could a team be developed?

School curriculum

Religious Education is the obvious subject with which clergy and churches engage. This can be done both by going into classrooms and assisting with specific topics, and by inviting schools to bring classes to visit the church. You can act out baptisms, communions and weddings, and allow children to go everywhere in the building, to touch, feel and experience the place as a living centre of worship. Have church members (suitably ISA / CRB checked) present to act as guides, and to answer questions.

There are wonderfully creative programmes put on by some churches to help children engage with the story of Holy Week, or Christmas, or to discover why Harvest is important as a festival. Events like Scripture Union's *Lifepath* and Gloucester Diocese Pilgrimage Days are fantastic resources to use. For assemblies, RE and other curriculum areas there are brilliant downloadable resources available like Damaris' Assemblies & RE lessons online, SU's *SchoolsLive*, BRF materials and the

Stapleford Centre publications. Introduce the schools to these and perhaps give them as a gift.

This engagement with the curriculum can be through regular or one-off visits. The simple point is there are many ways in which the local church can serve and help schools deliver their responsibilities to cover a wide-ranging curriculum.

Enterprising churches will put downloadable lesson plans, pictures, and ideas on their church website to add to the value of visits made into and from the school. It only needs one person who knows how to create web-based resources working with someone who understands the school curriculum.

Churches can also help secondary schools with careers advice by asking church members to talk and be quizzed

Think about...
In what aspects of the curriculum does your church already engage? What new areas might be possible?

about their varied careers – far better than a web search or online video.

Being a governor

Being a school governor is challenging and demanding in terms of time and of keeping up to speed with government regulations and initiatives. The governing body has a crucial role in the running of the school as a critical friend, especially to the head teacher. Governors do not just attend main governing body meetings but will be on a committee or two as well and will ideally drop in and visit the school in action at least once every half-term. They often take a particular interest in one area of the curriculum. There is always a need for particular expertise in finance, buildings, health and safety and child development. People become governors as parents, community leaders, local business people and local politicians. Every church ought to be encouraging at least some of its members to get involved in this way in all types of schools. Contact the schools directly, or the local education authority, to get good local information.

Becoming a staff member

Schools have all kinds of staff: teachers, teaching assistants, nursery nurses, cleaners, cooks, lunchtime assistants, secretaries, bursars, and others who often assist across several schools like Education Welfare staff, school nurses and gardeners. Many have started out as voluntary helpers and developed a longing to become more involved.

Teaching is extremely hard work, but is an astonishingly rewarding career. Churches should be encouraging people to consider teaching and other aspects of education as worthy careers to pursue. They should support all people who work in schools through prayer, understanding the demands and pressures, and offering practical support.

World links

All schools are now expected to develop links with schools in other parts of the world. This aids children's understanding of life in other nations and cultures. It encourages awareness of the strengths, gifts and needs of others. Links can be made through use of the Internet, emails, phone contact, letter writing, visits or teacher exchanges. They can be hard to maintain effectively, but where they work they are brilliant. Some of the best are where a community or church, or both working together, all make links with the same community. So the local school links to the school and the church links to the church. In this way, whole communities make connections, support and learn from one another. There are many examples where the church has led the way in helping schools, and communities, develop and maintain these links. The potential for more is immense.

Think about...
What world connections do your local schools have? Do your churches have? Can they be connected? How can these develop further?

Wrapping it up

Schools have become the focus of our local communities in many ways. With the Extended Schools Programme, and the inclusion in the curriculum of more social and moral education, schools are being asked to do more and more by government, the community and parents. They deserve, and demand our encouragement, support and help. There is no greater support for anyone or anything than placing them in God's hands and seeking God's blessing on them. So pray for your local schools, and find ways of getting every local church stuck into the life of every local school.

'…you will shine among them like stars in the sky as you hold firmly to the word of life' (Philippians 2:15,16).

In reality…
Burley is a village in the heart of the New Forest. The local Anglican Church is a little distance from the village centre. However, they developed some great engagement with the local community in relation to children and young people – all done by volunteers. Nearly all are over fifty, several well into retirement age, and the majority are women.

The church in Burley has simply responded to a community need – expressed by the young people themselves. The church has opened up its facilities for the young people to use on a regular basis. There is no other provision in the village for young people. A Wii has been purchased; there's a small pool table; food and drink are always on offer; there is space to sit and chat; sometimes cooking and craft activities happen. Occasionally trips out are arranged. There is also a football team. Instead of thinking about what they don't have (eg young leaders, a big budget) they have, under God, responded with what they do have. They have also had an impact on the small local primary school. In spite of some initial suspicion, patience and prayer have paid off and relationships between school and church have hugely developed.

Patient faith and a passionate commitment to the Lord and to the community have reaped rewards.

In the previous two chapters there have been many suggestions for how we can serve young people in our communities. We've looked at the church's involvement in the key areas of family and schools. Yet there are many other ways in which a local community, and the children and families within it, can be shaped by the good news of God in Jesus Christ as our opening story illustrates.

Think about...
How are you already engaging with the wider community of children?

Take a look at the Bible

'People were bringing little children to Jesus for him to place his hands on them, but the disciples rebuked them. When Jesus saw this, he was indignant. He said to them, "Let the little children come to me, and do not hinder them, for the kingdom of God belongs to such as these. Truly I tell you, anyone who will not receive the kingdom of God like a little child will never enter it." And he took the children in his arms, placed his hands on them and blessed them.' (Mark 10:13–16)

These young children are simply brought by community members to Jesus. The disciples are not sure about it, but Jesus is. He is furious with the disciples for turning these children away. But once he has welcomed them and blessed them, Jesus hands them back into the care of their parents and community.

The early church saw its primary witness as being Christ's community living in the midst of the wider community. They did preach and teach but for the most part they got on with their daily work, sought to do good to all and allowed their lives, both individual and corporate, to speak of the transforming love of Jesus (see 1 Thessalonians 3:9–12; 5:12–22; 2 Thessalonians 3:6–13; 1 Timothy 2:1–6). They were a people committed to the kingdom of God, that is, God's rule and reign. This kingdom is not confined to a part of life, it is about all of creation; it is about God's will being done on earth as it is done in heaven. It is about truth, justice, and wholeness; the total well-being of people in the midst of all of God's creation.

So we are to be concerned with people's salvation and long for all to enter into a living relationship with God through all that Jesus achieved at the cross. But God's salvation is so much bigger than simply snatching some individuals from the fires of hell. The cross of Jesus is about the renewal of all things; the end of unjust regimes; the redeeming of all creation. It is this big message that we are called to live and share (see Colossians 1; Romans 8). This must mean we engage with the communities in which our churches are set.

Think about...
How big is the good news you want to share with your community?

Practical ideas

Clubs and activities

Church-based activities like parent / carer and toddler groups, children's and youth clubs and holiday clubs now have a vital part to play in ministry to the wider community.

Toddler groups offer space for parents and carers to meet one another and chat over tea and coffee. They offer a safe space for small children to experience interaction with their peers. Well-presented Bible stories, simple songs and prayers, and linked craft activity can all be a part of the programme and will be widely accepted by people of all faiths and none.

From these, some churches have developed more specific worship events during the week for parents and toddlers. These are always interactive and short. They include all the elements of worship expected in a 'Sunday service' – music and song, stillness, prayers (saying sorry, thank you and please), listening to the Bible being read, thinking about what God is saying to us through it.

One of the most exciting developments in recent years for families worshipping together has been Messy Church. With its hospitality, creativity and community it has enabled many to worship for the first time, or to re-discover worship in new ways. Check it out.

Clubs range from simply being a safe place to play, through to those with more overt Christian content. One of the best in the latter category is the wonderful Kidz Klubs that started with Bill Wilson's Metro Church in New York. They are high energy events requiring a lot of staffing. They are also highly successful because of the deep commitment to home visiting that takes place every week in between the Klubs. In the UK the best of these are run by several churches working together, as one church alone may well not have the people or resources to sustain them.

There are also fine examples of clubs running with a specific focus, for example: drama, music or dance. In many African settings the choir with its drumming, rhythmic singing and dancing has long been the prime way in which children and young people have been gathered together.

Sport too is a potential focus. Football may appear to be all pervasive (for girls as well as boys) but others prefer rugby, cycling, Frisbee, cricket etc. Many top football clubs had their origins in church teams. Let us not lose sight of the opportunities our own times present.

Uniformed organisations like Boys and Girls Brigade, Scouts, Guides and Church Girls and Lads Brigade continue to provide a fantastic range of exciting activities for children of all ages. Church connections to these groups should be maintained as strongly as possible.

Holiday clubs provide great opportunities for fuller engagement with children, and wonderful activities to fill some of the school holiday periods. The resources available through SU, BRF and others are first class. Where churches feel unable to handle running a whole week of activities, running occasional activity days proves a valuable alternative.

Think about...

How does your church serve local children through activities? Are there fresh ways of action that could be tried? How well engaged with local clubs and activities are church members?

As well as thinking about activities that the church might organise and lead, also consider if the church might offer its facilities for others to use. It's also vital that children from Christian homes engage in activities in the wider community and are not simply closeted away in church-based events. Undoubtedly, sometimes the light will shine more brightly if church members get stuck into local clubs and activities and allow their lives to speak of God's loving ways.

Local facilities

A local church sometimes has good facilities. It has been great to see more and more churches try to gear their buildings for wider community use over recent years. It's not appropriate to try to turn all church buildings into community centres, but all can and should be used for as wide a range of activities as possible that are suitable and appropriate. There is a desperate need for quiet space in our busy, noisy world. Throw the doors open, let people, including children, in.

However there will always be more resource in national and local government, and in private business. Parks, gyms, sports centres, and public halls will be provided through this wider network. The Christian community should be concerned about proper provision for all people, especially in the areas of greatest poverty. This is a matter of justice. It affects the well-being of children, families and communities. Local people need to be engaged in thinking about such provision, and have a real sense of ownership over it so that it is valued and cared for well. Local churches can help the local community save, protect and develop local parks, design play areas, and create quiet spaces. They can help bid for money from local authorities and charitable trusts; they can help empower local people to act for the good of their local community.

In reality...
A cell group of a local church in Southampton took on the local recreation ground working with the local community and authority. The transformation has been astonishing and the witness to Christ very clear.

The welfare of children in the community often draws people together. As the church we should be at the very heart of this, not separated from it. Our allies will be people of other faiths, no faith, even those who are antagonistic to the church and think the message of the cross is total folly; but we should be at work for the best for all people in our neighbourhoods, and in the wider world.

The development of Sure Start Children's Centres is another aspect of local facility provision. The church can be an active partner in their development. Church schools are one obvious potential base. However, it's important that these are based in the best places to serve the whole community. Church members should be engaged in the local discussions about such projects and be active in such centres once they are open.

Child welfare and justice

This leads into the broader concern for child welfare and justice as a whole. The provision of local facilities is not the only concern. Are there local children's homes in your neighbourhood? How might church members volunteer to help with support for the children and young people living here? Is there an issue with runaway children? What about child prostitution? Are there refugee or asylum-seeking children in the area? Are there particular issues relating to children with disabilities?

These issues require expertise and skilled professionals. Thankfully, the church, particularly through organisations like The Children's Society, is at the forefront of working with such children, and advocating for their rights and their proper treatment. So simply supporting such organisations through prayer and finances is important. Yet there

may also be local opportunities for people to become involved voluntarily. These should be promoted carefully through the church.

There is a continual need for short- and long-term fostering, and for adoption. Churches should stay at the forefront of encouraging people to consider these as possible callings as one way of providing loving care for children in our society.

In the West, our protective approach to the nuclear family is a far cry from the open family we see modelled by our fellow Christians in many African, Latin American and Asian nations and which, it seems to me, is more typical of the families we find throughout the Bible.

In 2009 the Children's Society published 'The Good Childhood' report. It is full of revealing insights into childhood in the UK in the early years of the twenty-first century. It offers clear direction for a national debate on what we want a good childhood to be in the coming years. At least some of us engaged in Children's Ministry in church must engage in such a debate. The kingdom

In reality…

'Albert' lives in Rwanda and is seriously disabled. He did not start school until he was twelve because the family thought it would be wasted on him. He is top of his class. His father and mother have both died. The head of his family is his 22-year-old half-sister, who has a baby of her own. There are three others in the family. The Tumerere Project in northern Rwanda helps care for this family. They pray for and with them. They advocate on their behalf when others try to take the family land from them. They support in every way they can. Albert's life is being transformed by God's love in action.

Think about…

What matters of well-being and justice for children are there in your local community? In what ways is the church engaged or could be / should be?

of God demands justice and well-being for all children. We must work for a society in which it is safe for children to play on the streets, where infant and child mortality are continually in decline, children are allowed to be children, play is valued, housing is good for all and the values of love and trust are held uppermost. (See Isaiah 11:6–9; 65:17–25; Zechariah 8:5.)

Wrapping it up

Children are not isolated individuals. Families are not isolated units. We are all part of a wider community, nation and humanity. The well-being of all children is integrally bound up with the well-being of families, communities and nations. The church is not apart from this and should not stand aloof from it. God entered the world as a baby who lived out a full human life as part of a family within a community. He went through the suffering of the cross for us all. The incarnation and the cross demand that we become involved and get our hands dirty.

Are our hands dirty enough?

'From the lips of children and infants you have ordained praise'
(Matthew 21:16).

Everything we have talked about so far, developing work with parents
and grandparents, engaging with local schools, serving the local
community, will make a difference to the life of the church. It will shape
the way we pray and engage with the scriptures, our corporate
worship, our small group life, our use of resources – everything. In the
next three chapters we explore some further specific impacts on church
life, beginning with 'worship'.

Take a look at the Bible

Children express praise and thanksgiving to God for themselves. They
do so with words, songs, music, stillness and actions. On Palm Sunday,
as Jesus rode into Jerusalem on a donkey, the crowds cheered to herald
the coming of the King. Children were there joining in, right into the
Temple area itself. The children's worship caused quite a stir.

> *The blind and the lame came to him at the temple, and he healed*
> *them. But when the chief priests and the teachers of the law saw the*
> *wonderful things he did and the children shouting in the temple*
> *courts, 'Hosanna to the Son of David,' they were indignant. 'Do you*
> *hear what these children are saying?' they asked him. 'Yes,' replied*
> *Jesus, 'have you never read, "From the lips of children and infants*
> *you have ordained praise"?' (Matthew 21:14–16)*

Jesus was quoting from Psalm 8. The adult religious leaders tried to
silence the children. But Jesus pointed the leaders to the Scriptures as a
way of encouraging them to rethink their view of children and praise.

Now the children joined in for all kinds of reasons: some were encouraged by their parents or siblings; some were copying what they saw and heard happening around them. No doubt most did not understand the significance of the words they were shouting, but Jesus endorsed their actions and words as valid praise.

Children had been engaged in worship alongside adults throughout the pages of the Old Testament. They shared in the Passover in Egypt (Exodus 12) and were expected to engage in its celebration every year from then on (Exodus 12:25–28; Deuteronomy 6:20–25). Children took part in the weekly observance of the Sabbath and the annual celebration of the different Festivals (Leviticus 23; Numbers 28,29; Deuteronomy 16). The Feast of Tabernacles, when everyone camped outside for a week, must have been particularly exciting for the children.

In the New Testament, Luke's Gospel gives us the picture of families going up to Jerusalem for Passover (Luke 2:41–52). In the epistles there are not many specific references to children. However, those in Paul's letters to the Ephesians and the Colossians are significant. We have to remember that these letters were delivered by hand and read out aloud to the assembled congregation, most of whom would not be able to read. Children therefore heard all that Paul wrote. They heard the wonders of what God has done in Jesus Christ. They heard about the kind of lifestyle that flows from belonging to Christ:

Follow God's example, therefore, as dearly loved children and live a life of love, just as Christ loved us and gave himself up for us as a fragrant offering and sacrifice to God' (Ephesians 5:1f).

In this broader context they heard the words specifically directed to them as children: *'Children, obey your parents in the Lord, for this is*

right' (Ephesians 6:1).
Immediately after this they
heard Paul's instruction to their
fathers: *'Fathers, do not
exasperate your children;
instead, bring them up in the
training and instruction of the
Lord'* (Ephesians 6:4). Children were
present to hear these words read. They were worshipping, and
learning, alongside the adults.

Think about...
Take time to reflect on some of the Bible
passages quoted above. What picture of
children in worship emerges?

Practical ideas

Welcome and ethos

We need to see children as equal worshippers when we gather
together for worship. In our regular worship we should expect children
to participate, and value their contribution.

This will have implications for every aspect of our worship, but
particularly for the feel and ethos that we create. Does a young mum
feel welcome and at ease with her baby during a service? If the baby
cries out does she feel embarrassed or supported? If she discreetly
wishes to feed her baby (perhaps to help keep him quiet) whilst staying
in the pew, does she feel this is understood? If Dad decides that the
best thing is for the baby to have a five-minute break
outside, is the departure and re-entry seen as disruptive
or accepted? If the parent feels at ease, then the baby
will. Welcoming the newest infant is all about making
the parent(s) feel welcome. A look or an action speaks
a thousand words on such occasions.

As the child begins to grow, will their need for activity be recognised, or will movement be seen as intrusive and interrupting? If the minister's daughter wanders up the front to sit on Mum's lap whilst she is leading the service, will it be seen as a family at worship together or inappropriate?

As the young family walk into church together, is it just the adults who are greeted, or is everyone made welcome? Are the children offered their own copies of the books, service sheets etc? Saying they cannot read will not do; it is the act of being treated equally which matters. Our welcome of all as they arrive sets the tone for the worship. It should mirror God's welcome of us. In churches where 'the Peace' is shared during worship we must ask ourselves, 'Is this expressing God's peace and welcome to all?' Or is it grudging or selective?

What happens after the worship is 'over' also reflects this welcome. Do people just chat with their friends or are new people welcomed and made to feel wanted? If refreshments happen, are they good quality reflecting God's goodness and generosity? Hospitality of this kind before the service is sometimes a better option. Make people welcome; that is what God wants.

As children grow, are they invited to become part of the team that welcomes others, shares in taking up collections, leads prayers, reads the Scriptures etc? Involve and engage them in any and every way possible, seeing them as equals. When children lead a song, or perform a drama don't set it up, or view it, as a performance; see it as one way in which they are contributing to worship. Applaud them if it seems right – but then applaud adults in the same way too!

Where we provide good things for children, like areas with soft, quiet toys, are we providing things that connect with the worship as a whole, or are they merely activities which distract? All the time we should be seeking to help children engage with God alongside their older Christian brothers and sisters.

Think about...
Are we expressing God's welcome in our worship? What practical steps could we take to improve this?

Liturgy

Then we must consider carefully the way the liturgy works with children. Please note every church has a liturgy. In some, it is written down in a book, in others, it develops by custom and practice. Liturgy, written or unwritten, involves the shape and content of our worship. The content is important, as is the language. All churches are guilty at times of using over-complicated language when simplicity will do. There is a proper place for good theological language, but it is not always the most helpful language to use. This does not mean we have to dumb down worship to childish language. It's not essential to understand everything, just to realise what's important and feeling that it is. Children grasp the drama of the service long before they understand the words involved. If they sense they are welcome and included they will handle lots of things that 'go above their heads'.

Hymns and songs

Hymns and songs have been part of the church's worship from its outset, building on our Jewish roots (eg Psalms; Isaiah 35; Matthew 27:30; Ephesians 5:19f; Revelation 5:9; 15:3). These can and should be 'solid' theologically. They will include the saying or singing of Psalms, the words of Scripture set to music, and the re-telling of Scripture stories in song form. We learn much of our doctrine from our songs. This does not mean they need to be complex; simply-worded songs can be very profound.

Physical movement with songs can aid the worship and learning. The use of 'signing' in songs is very profound and more connection between it and 'actions' ought to be made.

Music on its own, to aid reflection, prayer and adoration has an important and often neglected place. Children who play musical instruments should wherever possible be included in music groups, at least on occasions.

Prayers

Those that come from the heart matter as much as the well-crafted words of a collect, poem or intercessions. Well-chosen visual images to help with prayer assist many people of all ages to focus their praying. So too active prayers – like writing a prayer on a paper leaf and hanging it on a prayer 'tree'; using sticky notes on a board; or blowing bubbles and imagining the prayer rising to the Lord, knowing that when the bubble pops the prayer is heard – can work for all kinds of ages. Children are well able to help with, or even lead, the prayers of the whole church family.

Bible reading

This needs to be done well so that the sense of the passage comes through. Children are just as capable of reading with meaning as adults. All may be helped by some practice, and even some explanation. Having a brief introduction to set the context of a passage can often aid everyone in their understanding. Reading the Scriptures aloud is an act of worship in itself, and needs to be treated as such by all. In some churches the gospel is 'processed' to the lectern before the reading and then held aloft after it has been read. For many, this may be an unfamiliar and strange practice, but it is designed to say to everyone, 'This is important; listen very carefully; heed what you hear.' It may not be a practice you want to emulate but it is a valuing of the Scriptures that all should take seriously. Stillness and silence after reading, to allow time for the words to sink in is important for all ages.

Exploring the Bible

The tradition of the sermon is not one that I have any desire to see lost. Preaching is a God-given way for communicating God's Word. However, there are many varieties of styles of preaching, some of which are better suited to communication with children, and many adults, than others. Preaching can certainly be interactive; allowing for questions and comments from the congregation within it.

Think about...
How do you help children engage with the Bible?

Space can be given for people to talk with one another, or simply have time for personal reflection. Still or moving visual images help many with their understanding. There is certainly the danger of 'death by PowerPoint' in some places today, but that should not detract from the valuable use of visual images; for some, just having the headings shown visually aids listening and remembrance. Make the most of the growing range of downloadable materials available, such as the 'Tools for Talks' film clips from Damaris.

The Scriptures can also be explored through drama, dance and the opportunity for creative activity.

Think about...

Reflect on the differing aspects of worship outlined above. How are we helping children engage in all of these?

However, it is essential that this part of worship really is about exploring the Scriptures. It is not just nice stories, or a moral chat, or a chance to show off great visual effects or performance. The task is to engage all ages present with the Word of God in all its power. Everyone who is called to the responsibility to teach the faith needs to keep their eyes clearly on the ball of explaining and exploring Scripture together.

Learning styles

In all of our worship, and other activities, we must continually be aware of the different ways people learn. The times of collective worship and

peer group activities need to cater for visual and kinaesthetic (or active) learners as much as auditory and reading ones. They need to engage all our senses. They must recognise the power and value of music, art, drama, silence, and words. Worship which engages children should never be childish, but it should be child-friendly and childlike. Worship should always be filled with reverence, holiness and awe, but that does not mean it has to be boring or lacking fun, excitement and joy.

Peer groups do matter and are valuable. We will explore them in the next chapter. But let's make sure that the children grasp that they are not 'being sent out' during a service so that the adults can get on with their 'proper' worship. What they will do in their peer groups led by those with some specialist gifting in working with them is an ongoing part of their worship, just as what the adults do is an ongoing part of theirs. An adult sermon is itself a peer group learning event. It makes most sense for there to be clear connections between what happens when all ages are together and when there is separate peer group activity.

Think about...
How aware are you of different learning styles? How well are these applied in regular worship?

Holy Communion

I have long been a strong advocate of the admission to children Communion. This is not the book to rehearse all the arguments for and against. However, it is the place to put in a plea that, whether or not children share in Communion in your church, when they are present at a Communion it is done in a way which includes and involves them. The drama of breaking bread, pouring out wine, and sharing the bread and cup around the people speaks powerfully to children. So let them see it happening. Take some time to explain what is taking place. Explain why we confess our sins together – it is not just individual confessions but recognition of our corporate sin as well. Explain why we share the peace (if we do), as a sign of our belonging to one another in Christ. Explain why we stand, sit, kneel, lie prostrate (or whatever other postures we may use). Unsurprisingly, when this is done, lots of adults will say how helpful they have found it. Communion can be done very creatively (see the excellent *Creative Communion* by Margaret Withers and Tim Sledge.)

Holy Communion, Lord's Supper, Breaking of the Bread, Eucharist – whatever title we prefer, lies at the heart of worship in most churches. It helps us focus on the incarnation, cross, resurrection, reign and return of our Lord. Children should be a part of this great act; they should be fully involved in it.

Think about...
How are children engaged with Communion in your church at present? How might they be more fully engaged?

Wrapping it up

Children are created to worship. Their very nature as spiritual beings, whose faith grows as it is nurtured and formed in the home and within the community of faith, is to be worshippers of their Maker and Redeemer. It is all of our responsibility to help children be worshippers. Developments like Messy Church help us think about how we plan and run our worship in ways that include children fully. Within the context of local church life this will be above all else about the ethos and feel of the church community. It needs to be a community that reflects its Lord in welcoming children into its midst, valuing them, praying for them, encouraging them and treating them as equal followers and worshippers of Christ.

6

SUNDAY GROUPS

'Let the little children come to me ...' (Matthew 19:14)

Sunday Schools were 'begun' by Robert Raikes in 1780. From the 1950s onwards the 'School' tag was increasingly dropped to try and break away from a 'school' image. All sorts of imaginative names have developed alongside a widespread use of 'Junior Church' or 'Sunday Groups / Club'. The title can convey something of what the groups are about and give ownership of the group by the children (so why do children so rarely get to choose the name?). However, it is how they are led and organised, and what happens within them which is most important.

Take a look at the Bible

'To what can I compare this generation? They are like children sitting in the market-places and calling out to others ...' (Matthew 11:16)

'Let the little children come to me ...' (Matthew 19:14)

Every child is an individual, with their own personality, gifts and family. Yet there is also a commonality of growing up as a child. Childhood is experienced in very different ways across, and within, cultures but there is a common experience of being a child. As Paul noted, *'When I was a child, I talked like a child, I thought like a child, I reasoned like a child' (1 Corinthians 13:11)*. So it is right to think of times and places where children gather together as children, as peers. It is just the same for adults. Peer times have a rightful place in our lives and in our ministry with children.

The nature of Sunday groups today

Today, the vast majority of children in Sunday groups are from 'church' families. In some settings it is only 'church' children; in others there are a significant minority who come from other backgrounds. Some children will be there under some sufferance; others willingly. The likelihood is that there will be a wide range of abilities present. In many churches the numbers are relatively small, and each group may cover quite a wide age range. It is a high calling to lead any of these groups. (See *Top Tips on Working with mixed ages*)

Parents and the wider church entrust these children into the leaders' care. Such groups and their leaders can never replace the parents in their responsibilities for helping children learn the faith, pray with them and so forth. However, what happens in these groups can supplement and extend the input that is received in the home. These groups are not 'child-sitting' services. They are meant to be places of engaging with God.

So they should involve all of the elements that happen in worship.

These groups should be places of hospitality and welcome, music and song, prayer, and reading and exploring the scriptures. They should be filled with creative activity. This may not be the case every week but all these elements should regularly be present. Creativity is essential. So too is allowing the children to express things in their own way. Let them use their own words in prayer. Encourage them to share what they make of a Bible story or passage. Avoid the temptation to think, 'I'm the adult, so I know the right answer'.

Content and ideas abound through published materials. Now that Scripture Union has put its 'back' material on line as *Lightlive*, there is an absolute wealth of material available. You really can design your own lesson using ideas and activities that will suit your particular group of children. Never be afraid of trying out some of your own ideas as well.

Godly Play is a powerful way of engaging children creatively in exploring the Bible for themselves.

These groups need to be safe places. Every group should have a couple of leaders, suitably checked, and preferably trained. If young people have the gifting and desire to share their own faith with the next generation, encourage them by getting them involved in helping to lead. Always make sure health and safety are followed carefully. Know your children and their allergies etc, have your first-aid equipment to hand and ensure all equipment used is 'safe'.

> **Think about...**
> What is the 'feel' of our groups?
> Is our content good?

Continuity

Knowing the children touches on a major issue of today: this is the problem of continuity.

The nature of family life with separated parents, and other family living away, often means that many children are not at a group, week in week out. Leaders can never be sure how many or exactly who will be present from one week to the next. This can be very frustrating in preparing an activity. It feels like such a waste if you prepare for ten and only three arrive – or vice versa. It makes planning activities difficult

> **In reality...**
>
> Kidz Klubs involve visiting the children in their homes every week. This not only builds relationships but also offers follow up for children who do not turn up one week, and gives a chance to check out and remind child and parent about the forthcoming event. This means that week by week there is good knowledge of at least who is expected at the group.

in other ways: some require larger numbers; others work better with small numbers. Adaptability is therefore a key skill.

I advocate more home visiting by leaders of children's groups. Or, why not phone or text every Friday as a reminder and to ask people to let you know if they will be coming to the group. At least that way there might be some clearer indication of numbers to be expected.

The other side of the continuity problem comes with leaders themselves. It used to be the case that most leaders would be there every week. Now, more and more churches have rotas of leaders. The reasons for this – more people in employment, dispersed families etc – are clear. However, it does make building relationships with children and keeping any continuity difficult. There needs to be good communication between leaders from week to week where this happens. It might be helpful to consider greater use of a 'month on' / off' rather than a 'week on / off' pattern. This means one leader sees a set of sessions through, even if their helpers change, and the children have more continuity of leadership.

There is no substitute for continuity and consistency of leadership for building good, strong relationships with children. Churches need to take this very seriously in their planning of how leaders are used. It is the relationships which are, above all, crucial. I remember very little of what I was 'taught' as a child in the two Sunday Schools I attended in my childhood. But I still remember the three women who led them and their attitude to me, to other children and to their Lord.

Think about...
What continuity are you offering?
Are relationships with children being built well and safely?

Practical ideas

Raising and developing leaders

This issue relates to all areas covered in this book but follows on neatly from the above section. Quite rightly, national legislation means that anyone working with children is properly 'vetted'. In the UK, fulfilling the new Independent Safeguarding Authority (ISA) and Criminal Records Bureau rules is important before anyone begins to help with children's groups. This makes giving people an opportunity to 'taste and see' more difficult than it has previously been. However, ways of inviting people to 'taste and see' remain important. People are concerned about committing themselves to something if they are unsure what will be involved.

This is why it is valuable for everyone engaged in work with children to have some kind of simple role description. What will they commit to? What and who will they be responsible for? Who will they be accountable to? What training and support will be given? What reimbursement for out-of-pocket expenses will happen? Proper simple training, ongoing in nature, should be part of everyone's expectation. This can be done as separate sessions, or a regular half or whole day. Small pieces of training can be included in leaders' meetings. Training alongside people from other churches, whether organised locally, or by a denomination, or 'churches together' group is invaluable as is attendance at nationally arranged training conferences eg Children's and Family Ministry Conference. There is a lot of 'cross-over' training available through experience in schools and other places of work involving children. There is also the simple invaluable learning that comes from experience as a parent, grandparent, sibling or carer. If every leader is helped to reflect on their group each time they lead it, they will learn rapidly.

All ages should be encouraged to help with working with children – older leaders, well into retirement, should be encouraged alongside the development of young people. Everyone should review their involvement on a regular basis, but be well aware of the value of a long term commitment in terms of building relationships. The most critical question in raising and developing leaders is this: 'Do they like children and want the best for them?'

Then, for those in church who do not see working with children as part of their calling, recruit them as prayer partners. Have every group and its leaders prayed for by people in the whole church. Have individuals pray for specific children by name on a regular basis. Aim to have every church member committed to prayer for children.

Think about...
How are leaders raised up, trained and cared for in your setting?
How can you encourage prayer for children throughout the church?

Single-sex groups

There is a renewed awareness that there are appropriate occasions for groups to be for boys or girls only. Each needs good role models from men and women. Each sometimes needs space with their own sex. The question of this for boys has been very well explored by Nick Harding in *Boys, God and the Church*. Be prepared, therefore, to explore the possibility of single-sex peer activity at least on occasions.

> **Think about...**
> Might there be a place for single-sex groups in your setting?

Taking them away

Residential events can be a crucial part of children's and young people's growth in faith. Find ways of taking children away: church children and those with whom you engage in other ways. The resources provided

> **In reality...**
> 'Molly' loved the camp. She entered wholeheartedly into every activity on offer. What no one leading the camp realised was just how important 'Molly' found being there in developing her own relationship with God. She came from a 'clergy' household. She had more than her fair share of church activities. Somehow being away from home in a different setting gave her the chance to make up her own mind about Jesus Christ. Today she is married, has children and together with her husband is actively engaged in making Jesus Christ known in a very different nation and culture.

through Scripture Union Holidays and CPAS Falcon Camps, for example, are fantastic. They enable churches of all sizes to take away small or large numbers. The variety of types of event, the length and the cost (there is assistance available for some of these camps for the poorest families) mean it is possible to find things that are suitable for most children.

In reality…

'Freddie' is still a teenager. His background could hardly be more different from 'Molly's', socially and economically. Church-going was never part of his growing up. Yet he loved a church children's club and when the leaders invited him to a camp he, and his mum, leapt at the chance.

Over five summers, alongside the week-by-week work in the local club and the regular contact and support between the club leaders and the family, 'Freddie' grew to know more about Jesus. He returned to the camp as a junior leader… He struggles with church but Jesus is real for him.

Then there are outdoor pursuits and residential field study centres (some with a Christian foundation, others run by local authorities or other charities) that offer great ways of doing your own day, weekend, or longer event. Staying away together can be an enormous adventure. Relationships are built in these settings which go so much deeper than an hour or two each week in a club or group activity. Whilst away 'a temporary community' is created. Here children can see and experience the Christian faith being lived out before their eyes. Go on, take the kids away!

Wrapping it up

Think about...
How might you 'take the kids away'?

Sunday groups have been declining in attendance throughout the last century. There has been a particularly steep decline in the last twenty-five years. However, they remain important for many children and families. They must be well led and organised. Most importantly they must be seen as part of the ministry of the whole church, not just a way of 'looking after' the children. The best day now may not be Sunday at all; children's cell or home groups meeting during the week may be a much better option. The basic guidelines, however, remain the same. Done well, all such groups are a valuable part of how children come to, and grow in, faith in Jesus Christ.

DECISION-MAKING

7

'He called a little child, whom he placed among them'
(Matthew 18:2).

> **In reality...**
> St Luke's were in the process of seeking a new vicar. They had to create their 'parish profile' and everyone was involved in putting something together. The children were honest about themselves, realistic and visionary about their hopes and dreams and made comments relevant to all age groups, to the whole community, and the church community. They presented it clearly, and with humorous touches. One adult leader on reading it said, 'Let's just use this.' It certainly made an impact on the person who became the vicar. He was impressed – and is working with them on turning dreams and visions into reality. The children had played a full role as equal members in the body of Christ.

Take a look at the Bible

'At that time the disciples came to Jesus and asked, "Who, then, is the greatest in the kingdom of heaven?" He called a little child, whom he placed among them. And he said: "Truly, I tell you, unless you change and become like little children, you will never enter the kingdom of heaven. Therefore, whoever takes a humble place – becoming like this child – is the greatest in the kingdom of heaven' (Matthew 18:1–4).

The new emerging leaders of Jesus' community were prone to be full of their own importance (see Mark 10:35–44; Luke 22:24–30; John 13). They failed to grasp Jesus' conviction that service is God's way. So Jesus places a child in their midst to help them learn the lesson.

Immediately the presence of a child changes our perception and understanding. It is this truth which has gripped the Child Theology Network in recent years. What does the presence of a child in the midst do? It is not simply our understanding of true greatness, humility and entrance into the kingdom which is affected. The child in the midst re-shapes our understanding of creation, being human, sin, salvation and the body of Christ. (See *Through the eyes of a child* by Anne Richards and Peter Privett.)

The presence of a child in our midst should affect our decision-making life as a church. The ideas and opinions of children are important. They might be the ones through whom the Lord will speak to his people, as he did through Samuel (1 Samuel 3) or the refugee servant girl (2 Kings 5). At the very least, they should be helping shape the activities put on for them specifically. Yet how many children's group leaders really consult and listen to the ideas of the children whom they seek to serve? There needs to be a revolution in how children's voices are being heard in decision-making. In order to help children express their thoughts, traditional ways of working will need to change. Children and young people (and many adults) do not function in the ways which our committees, councils, conferences and synods tend to do.

Think about...

In what ways does the presence of a child in our midst shape our church structural life?

Practical ideas

Committees and councils

Many adults struggle with committees and councils because of the way these work. It is no wonder that children may feel the same. Yet in most primary schools now you will find a school council operating with representatives of every class, including Reception and Year 1.

In some schools there are further groups that might take a lead responsibility, for example, on making the school 'greener', or doing charity fundraising. One really good development I have seen has been a working partnership between the school council of a secondary school with its catchment primary schools, working on matters like safety, traffic, rubbish, and charities together. They also help in a great way with the whole transition from primary to secondary schools.

Gathering children's views

The Children's Society managed to gain the views of 20,000 children and young people as part of their Good Childhood Enquiry. They have developed a whole range of excellent skills and resources to help children and young people participate in decision-making and expressing their views. Their specific programme for churches is '*Leaves on the trees*'. The Diocese of Wakefield undertook a fabulous survey of church children's opinions on church life and purpose during 2008–09. The Methodist church is also developing excellent materials to help this process.

So why do most churches still think that children's views are difficult to gather? The tools are available. Surely as the 'consumers' of Sunday and midweek church groups, or church services, the children's opinions matter and they should be sought? Here are some ideas that work. You can pursue them more fully through looking at the websites of the organisations already mentioned.

Give a session to ask them...
Simply give part, or all, of a Sunday / midweek session to asking them, 'What do you like most about this group? Why? What do you like least about this group? Why? What ideas do you have for what we could do better?'

Agree the rules
Take time with the children to agree the 'rules' of the group. One camp with particularly difficult children did this right at the outset. There were hardly any discipline problems all week because the children held each other to their agreed rules – most of which were exactly those that the adults wanted to lay down, but because the children defined them they self-disciplined.

Not just talk
Use drawing and drama to help the children express their views, not just conversation.

Involve them in big decisions

When a church is faced with a big decision, like appointing a new minister, or extending the building, or changing its service styles, or looking at a big community project, ask the children to express their views, and take them seriously.

When you are appointing a new minister involve a small number of children and young people in the process of meeting and talking with the candidates. Many a head teacher will tell you that the most telling part of their appointment process was the time spent with, and questions asked by, the school council. Children sometimes see a side of adults that other adults miss completely.

Children's and youth councils
Some churches are developing children's and youth councils. These look at the same issues as the main church council. For this to be more than tokenism the main council must take seriously the views expressed.

Get them to make a PowerPoint
Make a simple video, or PowerPoint presentation of children's views to present to the adults. Get them to do as much of it as possible. (They may well be technically more competent and proficient than most adults anyway!)

Recognise their gifts
Children are members of the body of Christ so the Holy Spirit gives gifts to them, just like everyone else. It might be that a child is given a word of prophecy, or a word of wisdom, knowledge or discernment that the whole church needs to hear; but do not be surprised if they express these gifts in childlike words and ways.

Think about...
How are children's views and ideas being heard at present?
Are there ways of developing their opportunities to share in decision-making processes?

Wrapping it up

Children are fully members of the kingdom and the people of God; they are gifted by the Spirit and their gifts need to be used. They are not disciples-in-waiting but disciples-in-the-making, just like every adult disciple. They are growing and developing in responsibility, and must be helped to do so. They have opinions and ideas which matter as much as those of anyone else. So, we have to keep developing ways in which children's views can be expressed, heard and taken seriously by the whole people of God. This means that they should be treated equally and engaged in the decision-making life of the church. Where this happens they will know that they belong. They will grow in spiritual maturity, and will be equipped for future responsibilities as well as current ones.

THE WORLD

8

Seek justice, encourage the oppressed. Defend the cause of the fatherless, plead the case of the widow' (Isaiah 1:17).

In reality...

Throughout my growing up, images of poverty came largely from Africa or the Indian sub-continent. So when I first visited Russia in the early 1990s, I was shocked by the child poverty which I discovered there. My wife's Brazilian cousin works amongst street children in her home city. It is a scenario repeated across Latin America: children who sell themselves, or are sold, into prostitution to make a living, or who resort to stealing; children who sniff glue to bring some relief from the boredom, pain and helplessness.

All over the world there are children in desperate need of clean water, food, housing, clothing, and basic education.

Take a look at the Bible

'He defends the cause of the fatherless and the widow, and loves the foreigners residing among you, giving them food and clothing. And you are to love those who are foreigners ...' (Deuteronomy 10:18).

'If anyone causes one of these little ones – those who believe in me – to stumble, it would be better for them if a large millstone were hung round their neck and they were drowned in the depths of the sea... See that you do not despise one of these little ones. For I tell you that their angels in heaven always see the face of my Father in heaven' (Matthew 18:6,10).

The law, prophets and Psalms all agree that God has a passionate concern for the poor. Walter Brueggemann describes this as 'the God who comes bodied in Jesus is indeed like a she-bear who will let nothing of abuse, exploitation, marginalisation, or poverty come between "her" and her cubs.' (Vulnerable Children in *The Child in the Bible* ed Marcia Bunge, Eerdmans 2008)

The followers of Jesus cannot be content to be concerned only for their own children or simply the children of their own neighbourhood or nation; though rightly they must be concerned with these. There must also be a passion for the children of the world, and particularly those who are vulnerable. This vulnerability will often be through poverty, including the spiritual poverty which is often characteristic of the rich rather than the poor. Jesus' warning about causing harm or damage to his little ones is very stark. We still fail to adequately take it seriously.

> **Think about...**
> Take time to reflect on God's character as 'Father to the fatherless' and 'defender of the weak'.
> How much do we reflect God's image in this way?

Practical ideas

Developing partnership links
Every church should have some overseas interests or connections. Rather than everyone doing their own thing, it makes sense to help the children you work with join in with your church's existing international projects. Connections between church and school world links make sense where they are possible too.

Children will find it much easier to relate to another child, family or group of children. This is the appeal of many of the child sponsorship schemes. The best ones really do work with whole families and communities, not just the named child. But support of a specific project that works with children is another valuable route. This allows specific identification, but leaves the project organisers free to use any financial donation the way that they judge best. Whilst financial support is right and valued, prayer and knowing people are interested is just as important. Above all avoid any sense of this being a one-way partnership; we have much to learn from the children and families in other churches and cultures. We may be able to offer material riches but often they will offer us spiritual riches.

Keeping in touch is never easy. We have all the advantages of modern communication, and expect instant responses. These are not so readily available in most parts of the world. Also when you are deeply engaged in caring for the poor, it is their needs that must come first, not sending nice photos and up-to-date information to people in the UK. So patience is required, along with faithful prayer and support.

Working for justice for the world's children
There also needs to be a commitment to working for justice for the children of the world. Feeding and clothing the poor is simply dealing with the symptoms. Transformed trade structures, improved governance, significant aid and development support, and a proper tackling of climate change are all required to bring real transformation. The church should be as deeply involved as it can be in these affairs as well. The Millennium Development Goals are one clear place to start.

Connecting with UNICEF is key in this regard. Then there are the many Christian organisations with whom we can engage: Viva Network, Christian Aid, Tearfund, Micah Challenge, A Rocha are all great places to begin.

> **Think about...**
> Take time to reread the Rwandan story on page 43.
> How might your own church and children become more engaged with the children of the world?

Wrapping it up

Those who have engaged with me over the past 40 years know that at the centre of my children's ministry is this word passion. Commitment to justice at every level for children has been my own biggest journey. I've always wanted children to share a living relationship with God, through the Lord Jesus, that God brought me into as a 15-year-old. I am as committed to sharing the good news of forgiveness and new life through Christ as I've ever been. But the vision has become larger and deeper. It now embraces the total well-being of children and their childhoods. It is a concern for the children of the world. I believe this world vision is important for us all. It enlarges our vision for the children for whom we have the most immediate responsibility, those in our own families, our churches and our neighbourhoods.

We have thought about many true stories of God's love at work in children. It is God's love made known in Jesus that really makes a difference. It is our responsibility to share that love with the children of the world. Techniques, programmes, ideas and activities have their place but unless they are motivated and directed by the power of the Holy Spirit they are worthless.

My final top tips for those engaging with ministry to children are based on Jesus' words from Matthew 22:37–39:

Love the Lord your God with every ounce of your being and…
Love your child neighbour as yourself.
Welcome the children in Jesus' name.

TEN TOP TIPS

- Make prayer for children a priority.

- Run parenting / grandparenting courses and support groups.

- Get involved or support children in your local schools, community and another part of the world.

- Include and involve children in worship all the time.

- Involve children in church decision-making.

- Take the children away for a weekend.

- Develop a world perspective on children and childhood.

- Get involved in seeking a good childhood for all children.

- Become like a child.

- Welcome children in Jesus' name.

RESOURCES

Organisations

Church engagement
Bible Reading Fellowship brf.org.uk & barnabasinchurches.org.uk
CPAS www.ventures.org.uk/falcon-camps for Falcon camps
CURBS (Children in URBan Situations) www.curbsproject.org.uk
Damaris www.damaris.org/talkstogo for Tools for Talks
Godly Play www.godlyplay.org.uk
Kidz Klubs www.kidzklub.biz
Messy Church www.messychurch.org.uk
Methodist Church www.methodist,org.uk
Mothers Union www.themothersunion.org
Scripture Union www.scriptureunion.org.uk for holidays, *Lightlive*,
    holiday club resources and *Top Tips* series
SU Northern Ireland www.suni.co.uk
SU Scotland www.suscotland.org.uk
Urban Saints Energize http://web.energize.uk.net
Wakefield Diocese
    www.wakefield.anglican.org/support/childrenandyouth/index for
    'Transforming Lives' materials

Schools engagement
Bible Reading Fellowship www.localchurchlocalschool.org.uk
Child Theology Network www.childtheology.org
Damaris www.damaris.org/cm/home/secondaryrelol for RE lessons and
    www.damaris.org/assemblies for assembly resources
Gloucester Diocese www.gloucester.anglican.org/education for
    pilgrimage days

Scripture Union – www.scriptureunion.org.uk for *Lifepath, SchoolsLive* and *It's your move*

Stapleford Centre www.stapleford-centre.org for schools publications

Community engagement

Sure Start Children's Centres www.dcsf.gov.uk/everychildmatters

The Children's Society www.childrenssociety.org.uk for the 'Good Childhood' report

YMCA www.ymca.org.uk & 135 local YMCAs

Youth for Christ yfc.co.uk & 60+ local centres

World stories and engagement

A Rocha www.arocha.org

Christian Aid www.christianaid.org.uk

CMS www.cms-uk.org

Micah Challenge www.micahchallenge.org.uk

Scripture Union International www.su-international.org

Tearfund www.tearfund.org

UNICEF www.unicef.org for United Nations Millennium Development Goals

Viva www.viva.org

Books

A Child Sees God, Howard Worsley, Jessica Kingsley Publishers, 2009

A Good Childhood, Richard Layard & Judy Dunn, Penguin, 2009

All age Lectionary Services, Scripture Union, 2010

All age Service Annuals 1–4, Scripture Union, 2007–2010

All-Age Worship Lucy Moore, BRF, 2010

Boys, God and the Church, Nick Harding, Grove, 2007
Children's Spirituality, Rebecca Nye, Church House, 2009
Churches Linking with Schools, Howard Worsley, Grove, 2010
Creative Communion, Margaret Withers and Tim Sledge, Barnabas,
    2008
Local Church Local School, Margaret Withers, Barnabas, 2010
Not Just Sunday, Margaret Withers, Church House Publishing, 2002
One Generation from Extinction, Mark Griffiths, Monarch, 2009
Rural Children Rural Church, Rona Orme, Church House Publishing,
    2007
Special Children, Special Needs, Simon Bass, Church House Publishing,
    2003
The Bible (Narrative & Illustrated), WTL Publications, 2006 (Available
    online only at www.WTLBiblePublications.com)
The Child in Christian Thought, ed Marcia Bunge, Eerdmans Publishing
    Company, 2001
The Child in the Bible, ed Marcia Bunge, Eerdmans Publishing
    Company, 2008
The Vocation of the Child, ed Patrick McKinley Brennan, Eerdmans
    Publishing Company, 2008
Through the eyes of a child, ed Anne Richards & Peter Privett, Church
    House Publishing, 2009
Toddling to the Kingdom, ed John Collier, Child Theology Movement,
    2009
Top Tips Series Scripture Union, 2007–2010
Understanding God's Heart for Children, ed McConnell, Orona &
    Stockley, Authentic, 2007
Where Two or Three, Margaret Withers, Church House Publishing, 2004

More Top Tips titles to help with your children's ministry...

Mega Top Tips on Dealing with challenging behaviour

Understand some of the psychological, physical and emotional causes of challenging behaviour. Learn ways of helping children and young people to manage their own behaviour and be inspired to draw them to God.
Sue Brown and Alice Langtree
978 1 84427 531 1   £4.99

Running holiday clubs

Reach out to children in your local community and in your church. Practical advice and real-life experience to help you run a Bible-based holiday club. Think-about suggestions to inspire and help you grow your team.
Vicki Brackpool, Helen Franklin and Steve Hutchinson
978 1 84427 541 0   £3.50

Working with mixed ages

Practical advice and real-life stories – to equip you in your work with small groups with a wide age range. Top tips full of wisdom and understanding – to help you face the challenges of a mixed age group. Passion for the good news of Jesus – to inspire you in sharing your faith with children, whatever their ages.
Maggie Barfield and Terry Clutterham
978 1 84427 542 7 £3.50

Order from SU Mail Order
Phone: 0845 07 06 006 Fax: 01908 856020 Online: www.scriptureunion.org.uk